LIGHTNING
BOLT
BOOKS™

How Do Fire Trucks Work?

Buffy Silverman

Lerner Publications • Minneapolis

Lerner Publications Company
A division of Lerner Publishing Group, Inc.
241 First Avenue North
Minneapolis, MN 55401 USA

For reading levels and more information, look up this title at www.lernerbooks.com.

Library of Congress Cataloging-in-Publication Data

The Cataloging-in-Publication Data for *How Do Fire Trucks Work?* is on file at the Library of Congress.
ISBN 978-1-4677-9504-3 (lib. bdg.)
ISBN 978-1-4677-9679-8 (pbk.)
ISBN 978-1-4677-9680-4 (EB pdf)

Manufactured in the United States of America
1 —BP — 12/31/15

Table of Contents

Racing to the Fire!

Lights flash. Sirens blare. A fire truck speeds to a fire. It carries people and equipment to fight fires.

Fire trucks use powerful diesel engines to carry heavy loads. These engines change diesel fuel into energy that turns wheels.

Diesel engines are engines that run on diesel fuel. They are different from most car engines, which run on gas.

Pistons move inside the engine. Each piston is in a tube. A piston goes down. Fresh air fills the tube. The piston moves up and squeezes the air. Squeezing air makes it hot.

Pistons are sliding pieces that go up and down.

Fuel is sprayed on the hot air. The fuel explodes and pushes the piston down. The movement of all the pistons turns a crankshaft. It makes the wheels turn. The fire truck zooms!

Pumper Trucks

There are different kinds of fire trucks. One main kind is a pumper truck. These trucks carry water tanks. They can also suck water from a hydrant or a lake.

Pumper trucks can suck extra water from fire hydrants if they need to.

A firefighter starts the **pump** on a pumper truck. It has its own diesel engine. When the engine is on, a part inside the pump starts to spin.

The water in a pumper truck's tank helps put out fires.

The firefighter flips a switch. This opens a valve between the pump and the water tank. Water from the tank flows into the pump. The pump shoots water out.

Other firefighters pick up hoses that are on the truck. The firefighter who controls the pump turns on the hoses.

Fire hoses shoot powerful streams of water.

If firefighters need more water, they can drag a big hose to a fire hydrant. The hydrant is connected to underground pipes.

You may have seen hydrants like this near your home or school.

A firefighter connects a hose between the hydrant and the truck. The firefighter opens the hydrant. Water gushes into the pumper truck. The pump pushes water to other hoses.

Pumper trucks also carry foam. Foam can put out gasoline fires. Foam coats a burning car. Air cannot reach the fire, so the fire goes out.

This firefighter sprays foam to fight a fire.

Ladder Trucks

Ladder trucks are another main kind of fire truck.

Ladders on these trucks help firefighters reach fires in tall buildings.

Do you see the ladder on this truck?

A firefighter pulls a joystick to raise the ladder. Pulling the joystick sends oil into a tube attached to the bottom of the ladder. The tube has a steel rod inside it. The oil pushes the rod out. The rod makes the ladder go up.

This ladder is all the way up!

The firefighter pulls another joystick to make the ladder longer. The ladder has three sections. The narrower sections fit inside wider ones. The sections pull out like a telescope.

A fire truck's ladder has three sections.

The ladder also moves to the left or the right.

A motor powers these movements. Gears rotate and the ladder moves.

This ladder can move to wherever it is needed.

The truck needs extra support for its heavy ladder. Outriggers keep the truck from rolling over. Outriggers are metal parts that stick out of the truck to balance it.

Outriggers fit in the sides of the truck when firefighters aren't using them.

This pipe can spray water on fires in high places.

A pipe is attached to the side of the ladder. It is as long as the ladder. The pipe sprays 1,000 gallons (3,785 liters) of water a minute. That's enough water to run a shower for more than six hours!

Room for the Crew

The driver sits at the front of the truck. The captain sits right next to the driver. The captain wears a radio headset to speak to other firefighters.

The captain is the head firefighter. Captains give directions to other firefighters.

The jump seat is behind the captain. More firefighters sit there. They listen to the captain through their headsets.

This is the jump seat.

Air packs like this bring fresh air to firefighters.

Air packs are stored behind the jump seat. Firefighters put on the air packs. They help the firefighters breathe in smoky buildings.

Toolbox on Wheels

Lockers in fire trucks hold tools for fighting fires. Some lockers hold extra hoses. They are folded so firefighters can quickly pull them out.

Lockers like these hold firefighting supplies.

Look at all the nozzles in this locker! Some nozzles spray a hard stream of water. Others spray mist. Nozzles can mix foam and water if both are needed to fight a fire.

Firefighters rescue people trapped in cars and buildings. These tools cut away cars and walls.

Fire trucks carry equipment to help sick people. Fire trucks carry oxygen tanks and equipment to start a person's heart. They are ready for emergencies.

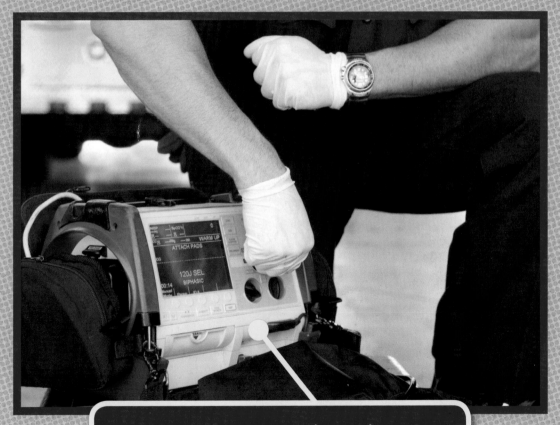

Thanks to special tools and lots of bravery, firefighters help people every day.

Diagrams

Pumper Truck

hose that connects to fire hydrant

hose

diesel engine

wheels

Ladder Truck

ladder

pipe

outriggers

wheels

diesel engine

Fun Facts

- A pumper truck carries 500 to 1,000 gallons (1,893 to 3,785 liters) of water. A tankful of water is heavy. A large tank of water weighs about as much as 146 eight-year-olds!

- A fire truck's lights, sirens, radios, and computers need power. Wires connect them to batteries. There are hundreds of feet of wires in a fire truck.

- Airports have special fire trucks made to stop fires on planes. These fire trucks use foam to smother burning fuel. The trucks are lighter than other fire trucks. They can race to a fire and save passengers.

Glossary

crankshaft: a long metal piece that connects a vehicle's engine to its wheels and helps them turn

diesel: a type of fuel and an engine powered by this fuel

nozzle: a short tube put on the end of a hose that controls the way water or foam flows out

outrigger: a part that sticks out of a vehicle to help it stay balanced

piston: a sliding piece that moves up and down inside the engine, changing chemical energy into motion

valve: a device that controls the flow of liquid by opening and closing

Further Reading

Aloian, Molly. *Fire Trucks: Racing to the Scene.* New York: Crabtree, 2011.

Bellisario, Gina. *Let's Meet a Firefighter.* Minneapolis: Millbrook Press, 2013.

Hanson, Anne E. *Fire Trucks in Action.* Mankato, MN: Capstone, 2012.

National Geographic Channel: Fire Trucks
http://channel.nationalgeographic.com/ultimate-factories/videos/fire-trucks

Science of Fire
http://www.firesafekids.org/science.html

Sparky the Fire Dog—Fire Trucks
http://www.sparky.org/firetruck/index.htm

Index

Photo Acknowledgments

The images in this book are used with the permission of: © iStockphoto.com/ryasick, p. 2; © iStockphoto.com/PJPhoto69, p. 4; © selbstr/Wikimedia Commons/(cc 3.0), p. 5; © Krasowit/Shutterstock.com, p. 6; © Greg K__ca/Shutterstock.com, p. 7; © Suzanne Tucker/Dreamstime.com, p. 8; © iStockphoto.com/Johncairns, p. 9; © iStockphoto.com/NoDerog, p. 10; © Joshua Kruger/flickr.com (cc 3.0), p. 11; © iStockphoto.com/Nancy Nehring, p. 12; © iStockphoto.com/studio2f, p. 13; © David R. Frazier Photolibrary, Inc./Alamy, p. 14; © iStockphoto.com/aluxum, p. 15; © Pierre Rochon photography/Alamy, p. 16; © Rob Byron/Shutterstock.com, p. 17; © Patrick Feller Follow/flickr.com (cc 3.0), p. 18; © Jim Parkin/Shutterstock.com, p. 19; © Cary Ulrich Photography/Alamy, p. 20; © Gaetano/CORBIS, p. 21; © iStockphoto.com/ollo, p. 22; © iStockphoto.com/tatajantra, p. 23; © iStockphoto.com/matsou, p. 24; © iStockphoto.com/ChiccoDodiFC, p. 25; © Joe Loong Follow/flickr.com (cc 3.0), p. 26; © iStockphoto.com/leezsnow, p. 27; © Laura Westlund/Independent Picture Service, p. 28; © iStockphoto.com/hkeita, p. 29.

Front cover: © Lee Cannon/flickr.com (cc 2.0).

Main body text set in Johann Light 30/36.